More time with God

What's God like?

John's Gospel Robert Willoughby | **Psalms 1–41** Elaine Carr

Also in the **Bible Max** series:
Journeys with God includes series on Genesis by David Bruce and Ruth by Helen Warnock.

© Scripture Union 2007
First published 2007

ISBN: 978 1 84427 283 9

Scripture Union, 207–209 Queensway, Bletchley, Milton Keynes, MK2 2EB, England
Email: info@scriptureunion.org.uk
www.scriptureunion.org.uk

Scripture Union Australia, Locked Bag 2, Central Coast Business Centre, NSW 2252
www.scriptureunion.org.au

Scripture Union USA, PO Box 987, Valley Forge, PA 19482
www.scriptureunion.org

Scripture quotations, unless otherwise indicated, are taken from the HOLY BIBLE, NEW INTERNATIONAL VERSION. Copyright © 1973, 1978, 1984 by International Bible Society. Anglicisation copyright © 1979, 1984, 1989, 1995, 1996, 2001. Used by permission of Hodder & Stoughton Ltd.

All rights reserved. No part of this publication may be reproduced, stored in a retrieval system, or transmitted in any form or by any means, electronic, mechanical, photocopying, recording or otherwise, without the prior permission of Scripture Union.

British Library Cataloguing-in-Publication Data.
A catalogue record of this book is available from the British Library.

Printed in China by 1010 Printing International Ltd

Cover design by Wild Associates Ltd

Internal page design by Creative Pages: www.creativepages.co.uk

Scripture Union is an international Christian charity working with churches in more than 130 countries providing resources to bring the good news about Jesus Christ to children, young people and families and to encourage them to develop spiritually through the Bible and prayer. As well as coordinating a network of volunteers, staff and associates who run holidays, church-based events and school Christian groups, Scripture Union produces a wide range of publications and supports those who use our resources through training programmes.

CONTENTS

Introducing... 4

JOHN'S GOSPEL: GOD LIVING AMONG US

The big picture 6

1. Introducing Jesus 9
2. Jesus answers questions 12
3. Three miracles 15
4. Jesus at the feast 18
5. Insiders and outsiders 21
6. Matters of life and death 24
7. Getting ready to leave 27
8. Absence and presence 30
9. Given for us 33
10. Lord of life 36

Bird's eye view 39

PSALMS 1–41: WHAT'S GOD LIKE?

The big picture 42

1. Our awesome God 45
2. The God who listens 48
3. The God you can trust 51
4. God of action 54
5. The God who longs to bless 58

Bird's eye view 61

INTRODUCING...

BIBLE MAX

More time with God

The **Bible Max** series aims to help you get the big picture of God's story as you read big chunks of his Word as part of an extended time with God.

Perhaps you have tried using Bible notes which give you a short passage to read each day. But, like lots of people, you may find it hard to keep going with daily Bible-reading times because life is too busy. Shorter passages may not make much sense out of context if you've forgotten what you were reading a few days before. **Bible Max** will help you read and immerse yourself in longer bits of God's Word including whole Bible books.

You might want to use **Bible Max** for longer regular reading, setting aside half an hour or more every so often. Or, you might use it for special times away from everyday commitments, for example, on holiday, days off or even for a retreat day. Although the material is written mainly with individuals in mind, you may also enjoy using it with others. But it's not just a question of knowing more about the Bible. **Bible Max** means spending more time with God. Each session offers suggestions and questions to help you talk with and grow in your relationship with him.

'The big picture' introduces each series, giving you some idea of where the Bible book fits into the big picture of the Bible and God's big story. Then there are several reading sessions with suggestions to help you into the Bible passages and to reflect on how it might connect with your own life today. Each series concludes with 'Bird's eye view' – a section to help you reflect on what you've read and then think about what it might mean for you. There's also lots of space for your own journaling as you're reading, where you can make a note of things God is saying to you – if you like to do this.

Different section headings are there to help you through each session with the Bible material. But don't feel you need to stick with the order suggested. Pick and choose what's helpful for you. Miss out a section, read more, read less! Relax – and see where God leads you as you spend time with him.

WHAT'S GOD LIKE?

What's God like? includes two series – one on John's Gospel and one on Psalms 1–41. **John's Gospel: God living among us** helps us discover more about God as we read about the life of his Son, Jesus, as recorded by John. **Psalms 1–41: What's God like?** takes a more personal look at what God is like as we meditate on the words of the psalms. The two Bible books are different in their styles and purpose and this is reflected in the different approaches taken by the writers.

As you read, reflect and pray, our prayer is that you will be greatly encouraged as you discover more about what God is like and grow in your relationship with him.

We'd love to hear how you get on with **Bible Max**. Please email us at: biblemax@scriptureunion.org.uk

About the writers…

Robert Willoughby lectures in the New Testament at the London School of Theology. He is the father of two grown-up children and, in his spare time, enjoys reading, music and sport.

Elaine Carr, when not with her young daughter, is responsible for resourcing the midweek groups at her local church.

JOHN'S GOSPEL: GOD LIVING AMONG US

The Big Picture

John gives us an account of Jesus' life and ministry which is quite different from those you'll find in the Gospels of Matthew, Mark and Luke. His perspective is outside of time and starts at the beginning of creation with Jesus the Word being involved in the act (John 1:1–3). John goes on to say that, in Jesus, God's Word came to live in his creation for a short while among human beings as one of us (1:14). Throughout his Gospel, John assumes that you'll know all the story already and will be able to stand back and reflect on it carefully.

You won't find some of the famous parts of the life and teaching of Jesus in John. He leaves out a lot – like the story of the nativity, the Sermon on the Mount, the account of the transfiguration, the breaking of bread at the Last Supper. John has his own agenda. Be open to what he wants to say, and the way in which he says it.

GETTING STARTED

Before reading John's Gospel it's worth refreshing your memory about the main events of the life of Jesus as told in one of the other Gospels (Mark is the shortest!). Then, as you read John, remain alert to the differences in his account. Or, if you prefer, just think the story through now. You could jot down an outline of the life of Jesus in the journal space, as you remember it.

JOHN'S GOSPEL

THINK ABOUT...

The first few chapters of John include lots of reminders of the beginning of Genesis, and not just the first few words! As you start to read John's Gospel, keep in mind that this is an account of new beginnings. God is doing a new thing.

John describes Jesus' main opponents as 'the Jews'. But clearly John can't be including all Jews since the disciples and many other followers of Jesus were Jews. It's been suggested that, for John, 'the Jews' represent the religious leaders who were more interested in safeguarding 'the old religion'. They were hostile to what God was doing when he sent his only Son to offer everlasting life to humanity (John 3:16).

John's Gospel includes lots of very vivid characters and seven gripping miracle stories which are related with great care. Look out for these high spots and take time as you read this Gospel to think about them. As you come across these in your reading you might like to note them down – then add something that you have learned about God from each.

BEGIN

The whole Bible tells us what God is like. That's one of its main functions. In John's Gospel this is concentrated in the person of Jesus. John implies, 'If you really want to know what God is like, here he is – God in human form!'

John 1:14 sums up the whole story. It's as though John can't quite get over his amazement that God came to live alongside us. John actually saw it himself – and the whole thing was absolutely glorious, right up to and including the cross, where the King himself was crowned, lifted up and enthroned. All of that is in view as you begin John's account of the life and ministry of Jesus.

Take a few moments to meditate on the words of John 1:14 now. As you think about Jesus, reflect on what his life tells you about his Father, God.

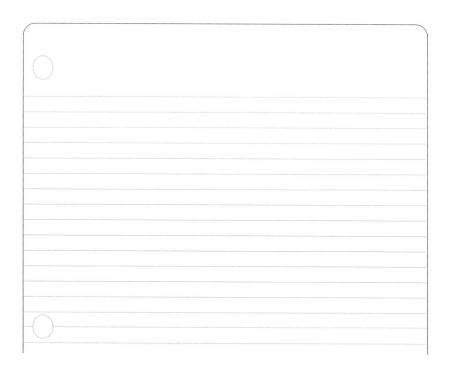

1 Introducing Jesus

JOHN'S GOSPEL

GET READY

Think about any famous person in history – for example Florence Nightingale, Nelson, Ghandi, Hitler – or your great grandparents! You might think about their life as a whole, weighing up their importance and overall effect on others. Alternatively, you might just think of particularly significant moments in their life when something important happened. These two chapters (as well as the rest of John) offer us both ways of looking at Jesus. Try to look out for them.

READ John 1,2

INTO THE BIBLE

These chapters have a number of clear sections. How would you divide them up? Try to ignore the divisions imposed by your own Bible!

John 1:1–18 is very like a poem. What themes set the scene for the rest of the Gospel? Which ones will you be looking out for?

John 1:19–51 Here, various disciples meet Jesus. How many ways do there seem to be of encountering him?

John 2 includes two stories which seem to be very important to John. Why do you think he tells them now?

GOD AND YOU

- John starts his Gospel with a majestic account of how God himself came to earth as a human being (1:1–18). Which of the big statements here have the most impact on you at present? Is it Jesus as the Light? Or the idea of his bringing life? The fact that he was rejected? The amazing thought of his being with people at all? His overwhelming importance? Why are these thoughts important to you at the moment?

- John is never actually called 'the Baptist' in this Gospel. Instead he is a witness to Jesus and points the way to him. Look again at what John says to the priests, Levites, Pharisees and others about himself and Jesus (1:19–34). How does this help prepare you for meeting Jesus?

- John the Baptist, Simon Peter, Andrew, Philip and Nathanael were left with plenty to think about as they met Jesus (1:35–51) – not least who it really was that they were meeting! Make a note of all the ways they describe Jesus. How do you like to describe him? And what do these descriptions really mean to you?

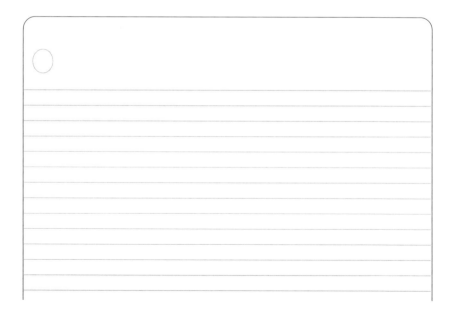

JOHN'S GOSPEL

- Clearly the changing of water into wine was more significant than just relieving a momentary social embarrassment! John says that Jesus 'revealed his glory' and the disciples began to believe in him (2:11)! Recall a significant time which helped you understand more about Jesus and helped your faith to grow.

- The 'cleansing of the temple' (2:12–22) happens later in the other Gospels (eg Mark 11:15–18), but John places it early on. Why do you think that might be? For the Jews, the temple was where you could meet with God. Where do you find God most perfectly expressed to you?

INTO ACTION

Such a magnificent portrait of Jesus leads us to worship. Take just one or two of the perspectives John gives us, or titles for Jesus, which you have thought about and meditate on them, turning them into worship, thanksgiving and prayer.

Extra

Read Isaiah 25:6–9 for a description of the future 'messianic banquet' to which the Jews were looking forward. Think about how Jesus brings such joy and celebration into your life and thank him. If you have a Bible dictionary do a bit of research into both this and the temple in Jerusalem.

2 Jesus answers questions

GET READY

We often say that 'comparisons are unfair' – but that doesn't stop us making them! In fact it can be one of the most productive ways of highlighting the characteristics of the two people concerned. This is nothing new. People have made comparisons between important people for centuries. This seems to be John's intention as he introduces the two main characters in these two chapters.

READ John 3,4

INTO THE BIBLE

Both these chapters, at first glance, seem to be conversations: between Jesus and Nicodemus, then between Jesus and the Samaritan woman. But look again carefully at the two chapters. What happens in the conversations?

Compare Nicodemus and the Samaritan woman in the way they come across as *people*. How does Jesus respond to them? Why do you think he treats them differently?

There are sections at the end of each chapter dealing with two other characters: John the Baptist (3:22 – 4:3) and the royal official in Cana (4:43–54). What do you think of *their* attitudes to Jesus? How do you think they grow in their understanding of him?

GOD AND YOU

- Do you ever think it would be good if God could give you a sign? Perhaps it would confirm your faith or provide direction. People have always looked for the sort of certainty that signs appear to offer. The problem is that you still have to decide what they mean! Read Nicodemus' opening comments to Jesus keeping this in mind (2:23 – 3:2). What would you have said to Jesus if you were Nicodemus? Would you be looking for further signs or evidence of his identity?

- Jesus sets a somewhat new agenda for their conversation from the one Nicodemus started with (3:3–15). It's one that goes right to the heart of Nicodemus' real need – for new birth. Ask God to help you to identify your own real needs as Nicodemus needed to do.

JOHN'S GOSPEL

- What, according to John 3:16–21, did Jesus principally come to bring? Read through these verses again. As you do so, think about how these words fit with your own life and relationship with Jesus.

- When John the Baptist reappears in the story (3:22–36), what do you think is the main point being made? John's example is very moving (3:30). Is it a challenge to you?

- Read again John 4:10–15. What do you think Jesus might saying about the Spirit in his image of the spring of water (4:14)?

- If Nicodemus fades out of the conversation in chapter 3, the royal official (4:43–54), like the woman in the preceding story, seems to 'hang in there' (vs 48,49). Do you think there is a sense in which God sometimes seeks to provoke a response *from us* before proceeding?

INTO ACTION

The Samaritan woman is different from Nicodemus in many ways. Jesus deals with her very personally. What do you think we can learn from his approach? In which ways could this encounter serve as a model for mission on a one-to-one basis?

What do you think we could learn about the nature of Christian mission from chapter 4?

Extra

John 3:16 is sometimes described as 'the gospel in a nutshell'. From what you know of John's Gospel and the rest of the Bible, try to express the gospel message in a single phrase.

3 Three miracles

JOHN'S GOSPEL

GET READY

Signs point the way, identifying people and places. Imagine yourself lost after dark in an unfamiliar city in a foreign country without a map. It would be a frightening experience. On the other hand it might be very satisfying to follow a map accurately and arrive in the right place without losing your way!

In the first half of John's Gospel and his account of Jesus' public ministry we're told about seven signs. We would probably call them 'miracles', but John calls them 'signs'. They point to something deeper about Jesus – who he is and what he came to do for humanity. Remember that Nicodemus was attracted to Jesus by his signs (2:23 – 3:2). Today, these signs invite us, as well, to look further and discover the reality to which they point.

READ John 5,6

INTO THE BIBLE

Here we find three miracles – 'signs': the healing of a man who had been lame for thirty-eight years (5:1–9); the feeding of the five thousand (6:1–15); and Jesus walking on water (6:16–24). Earlier we read about the two miracles in Cana (2:1–11; 4:46–54). Look out for the remaining two miracles in chapters 9 and 11.

The signs in these chapters provoke many questions from the group John calls 'the Jews'. How would you describe their reaction to what they have seen?

The discussions which follow the 'signs' (5:16–47; 6:25–59) are not always easy to understand. Read each chapter again and try to see why, at each stage, 'the Jews' object to what Jesus does or says. Their questions or misunderstandings (spoken or implied) frequently prompt Jesus to make further statements. Try to plot the way he moves from one assertion to the next and why he does this.

Extra

A Jewish debate of the time centred around exactly who was looking after the world when God rested on the seventh day of creation (Genesis 2:2,3). What do you think? How does this help you to understand John 5:16–23?

GOD AND YOU

- Read again the story of how Jesus healed the lame man at the pool of Bethesda (5:1–9). What does it tell you about Jesus and his Father, God? How does it speak especially to you?

- For the Jews of Jesus' day, working on the Sabbath could be regarded as a capital offence (Numbers 15:32–36). Should Christians 'keep Sunday special' today? How does this relate to the Bible's teaching about the Sabbath?

JOHN'S GOSPEL

- Look again at how Jesus moves from apparently breaking the Law (5:8–11) to discussing his relationship with the Father (5:16–18). What does Jesus actually say about this (5:19–30)? How do these verses challenge you about your own relationship with Jesus and his Father?

- Read through John 5:31–47 again. Jesus speaks of witnesses who give testimony to who he is. Who are they and how do they bear witness to Jesus? The unnamed one (5:32) is probably the Holy Spirit (14:15,16), also called 'the Counsellor' in John 14–16. What do these witnesses mean to you for your faith in Jesus?

- The feeding of the crowd and the crossing of the water recall the events celebrated at Passover (6:4). Read again the conversation after Jesus had crossed the lake (6:25–40). In what ways does Jesus challenge those around him (6:26–29)? What do you want from Jesus?

INTO ACTION

Chapter 6 continues the discussion about Jesus as the Bread of Life (6:35). Think of the various ways in which Jesus meets your deepest needs. How might he transform your life if you were really to take his words in these verses to heart (6:26–58)?

4 Jesus at the feast

GET READY

What kind of place do you find most atmospheric? An awe-inspiring corrie in the mountains of Scotland? A large international sports arena? A huge medieval cathedral? Somewhere quiet and dimly lit?

Sometimes an atmospheric place can be linked to a special event like a great musical performance or winning a trophy. The temple at Jerusalem during the Feast of Tabernacles was just such a place. There were crowds, religious fervour, memories of Israel's wanderings in the wilderness, a festival of candles and pouring water down the steps of the temple itself. To cap it all, imagine that a young teacher, whom some considered to be a prophet, is rumoured to be coming to town. Who is he? And how will others react?

READ John 7, 8

INTO THE BIBLE

Jesus always seems to be in complete control of things. Can you see any evidence in chapter 7 that Jesus planned his trip to Jerusalem very carefully?

'The Jews' and the crowd have many questions about Jesus in chapter 7. Make a list of them and note Jesus' responses (eg verses 15,26,35,41–42,47–48). Does he answer them directly or address the deeper questions which lie behind the issues they raise?

On the closing day of the Festival, water (often a symbol of God's Spirit; see also 4:9–15) would have been poured out. Perhaps this is what prompts Jesus to talk about the Spirit. What are we told about the Spirit and what he will do when he comes (7:37–39)?

Did you notice how the hostility of 'the Jews' has hardened (7:45–49)? What shows that they are in the process of rejecting Jesus 'the Light of the World'?

JOHN'S GOSPEL

GOD AND YOU

- Nicodemus makes the second of his three appearances here (7:50–52; see also 3:1–15, 19:38–42). Do you think he shows any sign of growth in belief? What do you think about the idea that people can grow into faith or even be seeking for quite a long time?
- Water is the first symbol connected with the Feast of Tabernacles, the second is light in the form of candles lit in celebration. What does it mean to you that Jesus is the Light of the World (8:12)? How do you feel about Jesus shedding his light into the dark places of your experience?

Extra

The Feast of Tabernacles was one of the Jews' festivals and lasted for seven days. Everyone was meant to live in 'booths', temporary shelters, reminding them of their journey through the desert to the Promised Land. Find out more in Leviticus 23:33–44.

- Many scholars think that the story about the woman caught in adultery (8:1–11) doesn't really belong here. However, it's another example of how the religious leaders were out to get Jesus (8:6). Yet he shows great concern for the woman. What does this tell you about God's willingness to forgive your sin? You might like to spend some time now confessing to God anything that is troubling you.
- The hostility of 'the Jews' described in chapter 8 is really unpleasant. What particular aspects touch you especially?
- Jesus is often forthright in his response, but here he is perhaps at his fiercest. Is this something you find disturbing? Or do you need to readjust your perception of Jesus? Remember, he wasn't condemning all Jewish people, only those who persistently rejected him at that time.

INTO ACTION

Ask God to give you the experience of the Spirit promised in 7:37–38.

How can you be the agent of Jesus' light to the world which you inhabit daily? What would it mean in practice and what effect would it have on others?

Extra

Water is a common symbol in the Bible. But what does it symbolise? Think through the story of the Bible (creation, Noah, the exodus, Jonah, baptism etc) and see how water symbolises a number of different things.

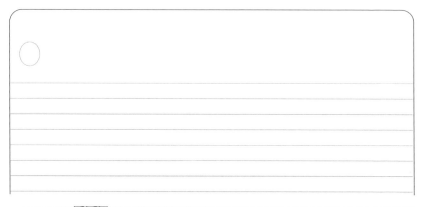

5 Insiders and outsiders

JOHN'S GOSPEL

GET READY

Would you describe yourself as an 'outsider' or an 'insider'? Or both at different times? Some of us relish either, or both, of these positions. Do you have a particular reason for sometimes feeling like an outsider – not really accepted by others?

At the time of Jesus, people with disabilities were treated very badly. Others tended to think that there must be some reason for people's misfortunes – perhaps a sin they or their parents had committed (9:1,2). This could lead to unbelievable cruelty and discrimination. The man born blind in chapter 9 is even used as a pawn in the Pharisees' attack on Jesus (9:13–34). In fact, the Pharisees try in vain to trip up both him and Jesus with their cleverness.

READ John 9,10

INTO THE BIBLE

How would you describe the man in chapter 9?

Make a note of all the places where light, eyes, sight, looking and blindness are mentioned in chapter 9. How does this story illustrate the statement made by Jesus in 8:12?

Do you find anything funny or ironic in the story?

How do you think the Pharisees must have felt by the end of their encounter with Jesus?

Look again at chapter 10. Try to break down the chapter into its major parts.

Jesus uses more than one word picture to describe who he is and what he's come to do – it's important not to mix them up. They are related but are not all saying precisely the same thing.

What do you think the sheep pen might represent (v 1)?

Chapter 10 is also about 'insiders' and 'outsiders'. Who would you say are the thieves, robbers and hired hands in 10:1,12,13? Jesus is clearly the gate and the shepherd (10:7,14). Where does he lead the sheep and where are they safe (10:27,28)?

GOD AND YOU

- Are there any ways in which you feel able to identify with the man born blind? What might Jesus be saying to you about any hard experiences you've had or difficult circumstances you're in?

- Do you think people like the blind man may be somehow more open to Christ's work in their lives than those more fortunate? See what Jesus said in Matthew 5:3–12.

JOHN'S GOSPEL

- What do you think of the picture of Jesus as the Good Shepherd in chapter 10? Does the chapter challenge any of the fixed ideas you might have had about your relationship to Jesus?

- There is a great deal about listening and hearing in chapter 10. How do you hear the voice of Jesus? What might he be saying to you through what you have read?

- Who are the real 'outsiders' in these two chapters? Do you feel compassion for them as well?

INTO ACTION

Do these chapters challenge you in any way concerning your exercise of Christian ministry to those less fortunate than yourself?

Does the picture of the shepherd and the sheep throw up any new ideas about church, witness and those outside the church which you could put into action in the weeks ahead?

Extra

In the Bible, God's people are sometimes described as sheep with God as the chief shepherd. Psalm 23 and Ezekiel 34 are examples of this. Look up and read one of these chapters if you've time now.

6 Matters of life and death

GET READY

The ultimate statistic – everyone dies. But, of course, it's much more than a statistic – it's the ultimate reality, and the presence of death raises questions and pain which at other times we prefer not to face. John chapter 11 is a climactic moment in the Gospel and you can feel the tension and the sadness, because most of us have shared the feelings of Martha and Mary.

Apart from the arrest and crucifixion of Jesus, it is in many ways the fullest and most developed story in all of the Gospels. Here we touch the deepest of human experiences. Take a little while to reflect on that in the light of your own experience and to be ready for how you might feel as you read. Chapter 12 is a kind of summing up of this stage of Jesus' public ministry, so you may be sure that we are coming to the climax of John's story.

READ John 11,12

INTO THE BIBLE

Do you think Jesus 'stage-managed' the situation to achieve a greater end in chapter 11?

Make a list of, or underline, all the places where human feelings are mentioned, including those of Jesus.

As people often do on such occasions, Martha has a complaint to make to Jesus (11:21). How does Jesus use this to lead her on to a deeper understanding of his life and ministry (11:23–27)? Look back to John chapter 4 where Jesus talks with a Samaritan woman. Notice how that conversation works in a similar way.

JOHN'S GOSPEL

The raising of Lazarus is the first climax of the Gospel but it also seems to be a final provocation to 'the Jews' (11:45–57). Why do they get so worked up?

When Mary anoints Jesus at their home in Bethany (12:1–11) it's a kind of preparation for Jesus' death (vs 7,8), something with which many of those close to him could not come to terms, including Judas. Why do you think this was?

The reasons for Jesus' incarnation and death begin to become clear from 12:12 onwards. John talks several times about Jesus being 'glorified' (12:16, 23, 41). What do you think this means?

GOD AND YOU

- Jesus' delay in going to Bethany forced Mary and Martha to put their grief into the wider context of God's purposes. Think of a similar situation you've been in. How has that affected your view of God and his purposes? How difficult did you find it to trust him? Why not bring any such situations you're facing, or painful memories, to Jesus now?

- At first, Martha thinks of resurrection as something which will happen to everyone at the end of time (11:23–26). Jesus has to correct her. How conscious are you that resurrection life has begun for you as a believer right now? What difference does it make to you?

INTO ACTION

Mission is a half-hidden agenda in John (eg 1:11–13; 4:39–42; 10:14–16; 20:21) and comes up here in chapter 12 in the shape of 'some Greeks' (12:20–26). How central should mission be to you as a Christian? Look at John 20:21.

Might the story of the raising of Lazarus help you bring comfort to anyone who has recently been bereaved?

Extra

> The last section of these chapters (John 12:37–50) rounds up some of the themes with which the Gospel began. Look back to John 1:1–18 and see how many things are mentioned in both passages.

7 Getting ready to leave

JOHN'S GOSPEL

GET READY

Setting off on holiday can be both exhilarating and worrying: what might we have left behind? Moving to a new job or starting a new phase in life can be wonderfully stimulating, but many of us find leaving, or starting, difficult and stressful.

The experience of bereavement covers not simply death but many other occasions of loss – for example, children leaving home (for both parents and children), redundancy, moving away from friends. John chapters 13 and 14 are like the beginning of the final episode of a favourite TV drama. It's all fascinating but a bit sad. Loose ends must be tied, threads brought together and a satisfying conclusion provided. From now on the pace slows down in John's Gospel – there is less action and more talk. Just a week or so of time is covered.

READ John 13,14

INTO THE BIBLE

Apart from Jesus, Simon Peter and Judas are the main characters in John 13:1–30. Compare their attitudes. Neither of them really understands what is going on. So how are they different? And why?

Jesus is very much the driving force again behind what happens. Can you see how he sets the pace and takes charge?

John 13:31 – 14:31 includes a long dialogue. Several of Jesus' disciples prompt him by asking questions (13:36; 14:5,8,22). What are these questions and how does Jesus answer them?

In chapter 14, when Jesus speaks of returning, do you think he is referring to his own second coming or to the coming of the Holy Spirit (or 'Counsellor')? Or both?

GOD AND YOU

- Jesus' actions in 13:2–5 are very intimate and would have surprised his disciples. Generally speaking it was servants who washed the feet of others. Imagine yourself in the place of one of the disciples. How do you think you might have felt? Uncomfortable, grateful, outraged, embarrassed?

- After his initial refusal to let Jesus wash his feet, Peter's eventual reaction is characteristically bold and wholehearted (13:9). Do you think Peter's reaction and attitude here are something for us to follow?

- Judas' betrayal is described in detail (13:18–30). Have you ever thought that you might have betrayed Jesus? How was that different from what Judas did?

JOHN'S GOSPEL

INTO ACTION

The emphasis in these chapters is on 'What next?' Jesus' followers have to get used to the idea that he's leaving and making provision for them in his absence. His provision is for us too.

What difference does it make to your life on a daily basis that you have a fundamentally different code for life from others around you?

What difference does your hope for the future make in the way you live every day?

What difference does the knowledge of being a friend of God Almighty make?

What difference does the presence of God's Spirit make to your life minute by minute?

Extra

Jesus says some key things to his followers about:

their behaviour (13:34,35);

their future hopes (14:1–4);

who he is (14:6–14);

the nature and ministry of the Holy Spirit (14:16–27).

Take each of Jesus' important statements about these and write a prayer expressing what they mean to you.

8 Absence and presence

GET READY

Think back to what it felt like when you started school. You left home and were finally in what seemed like the big, wide world with no one from home to do all of the usual things for you. Do you remember how you coped? Or what about starting a proper job for the first time? Perhaps the atmosphere seemed strange or even hostile. In both cases there was a brand new start: there were some things which continued, but a lot of things which changed.

In these three chapters Jesus develops his crash course for the disciples on the things which will really matter in the new start that's coming. It's a kind of farewell speech, rallying the troops, preparing them for battle. It's also a kind of handing over to the disciples. Fortunately for them (and us) he does not leave them to cope on their own!

READ John 15–17

INTO THE BIBLE

This is a long reading and it's worth breaking it down into chunks. Try this: John 15:1–17; 15:18 – 16:4; 16:5–16; 16:17–33 and, finally, chapter 17.

For some background to what Jesus says in John 15:1–17, look at Isaiah 5:1–7 and Mark 12:1–12. How do these passages shed light on what Jesus is saying in John?

Jesus never promised freedom from problems (Matthew 5:10–12). How does he now relate this to himself and his followers (15:18 – 16:4)?

JOHN'S GOSPEL

Are there any aspects of the Spirit's ministry as described in 16:5–16 which surprise you?

In many ways Jesus goes on to pull together what he has been teaching in these verses in 16:17–33. What are his main points?

Look at what Jesus prays for himself (17:1–5), his disciples (17:6–19) and for all believers (17:20–26). Do you notice any similarities or differences between what Jesus prays for each?

GOD AND YOU

- Jesus has already pointed out his own dependence on and obedience to the Father (eg 5:19,20; 14:28). If this is necessary for Jesus, it's no surprise, then, that his followers can achieve nothing worthwhile without him (15:4,5) – but with him there are even greater things to be achieved (14:12–14). Indeed the Father will do anything which is asked in his name (14:13,14; 15:16). How does this affect the way you run your life?

- No sane person goes looking for persecution, but how does this passage help you to be prepared for it should it arrive (15:18 – 16:4)?

- How do you think the Spirit led believers in the past? How does the Spirit lead you into truth (16:12,13)?
- Imagine yourself in the position of the first disciples as you read 16:17–33. How do you think you would have felt in those circumstances as Jesus spoke to you?

INTO ACTION

Think about the picture of the 'true vine' in chapter 15. If we take seriously the idea of believers being bound to Jesus like branches into a vine in God's vineyard, how might that change the way we feel and act towards them?

Are there any things in Jesus' great prayer in chapter 17 which you need to incorporate into your own prayer life? As you read it again, does it suggest to you any changes you need to make to the way you pray?

Extra

These chapters are a kind of 'last will and testament'. Jacob's words to his sons in Genesis 49 are a bit like this. How do these compare to what Jesus said here?

9 Given for us

JOHN'S GOSPEL

GET READY

Getting ready for a great event is important. You might be going out for an evening. Or maybe you need to prepare properly for a job interview or a presentation. The story of Jesus is reaching its climax. Everything has been preparing for this moment. The tension in the last few chapters has been building and time seems to have been slowing down.

READ John 18,19

INTO THE BIBLE

18:1–11 As Jewish leaders and soldiers come to arrest Jesus, who do you think is really in control?

18:28–40 Is Pilate completely out of his depth? Who is judging whom? Look out for any points of irony in these verses.

18:28 – 19:22 The kingdom of God is a key theme in Matthew, Mark and Luke, but only really appears in John's Gospel in John 3:3–5. Look at the discussion of kingship in these verses. Compare this with what Nathanael and the crowd said and did at earlier points in the Gospel (1:49; 6:15).

19:1–16 Jesus had talked before about this point in time as his 'glorification'. How is this reflected here?

19:16–37 Most writers today would have included all the gory details in their description of the crucifixion and death of Jesus. John's account, however, is very sparing. Why do you think he chooses each of the details which he does include?

GOD AND YOU

- **18:12–27** Compare the actions of Simon Peter and Annas. Why is it easier to sympathise with Simon Peter? Why do you think he denied knowing Jesus? Talk with God now about any times when you have had a sense of letting Jesus down. Does Simon Peter's experience shed any light upon that or help in any way?

- The cross is the climax of all of the Gospels. John prophesied at the outset, 'Look, the Lamb of God, who takes away the sin of the world!' (1:29). In John 6:51–58 Jesus says how his flesh and blood are vital for us. In 10:14–18 Jesus talks about himself as the Good Shepherd who lays down his life for his sheep, and then Caiaphas talks about how one must die for all (11:49,50; 18:12–14). How central to your faith is the fact that Jesus gave his life to take away your sins, a sacrificial lamb, dying instead of you? It's central to John's story. Talk with God about this now.

- Nicodemus reappears here (19:38–42). Look back over his previous roles (3:1–16; 7:45–52). What do you think he came to believe about Jesus? How does he develop in the story? Think about how your own belief in Jesus has developed.

Extra

> There is some discussion amongst biblical scholars about Annas and Caiaphas and who is being referred to as the high priest here. Find out more about them from a Bible commentary.

JOHN'S GOSPEL

INTO ACTION

In these chapters, Jesus is presented as a different kind of king. What might it mean to you, both personally and in your work, to acknowledge Jesus as rightful King over the world?

Christians worship a crucified King (John 19:19–22). Take time to think about your crucified Lord and offer him praise and thanksgiving.

Extra

John's account of the crucifixion of Jesus differs in certain respects from what we are familiar with in the Gospels of Matthew, Mark and Luke. Read their accounts too and note down what is different.

10 Lord of life

GET READY

What is the most surprising, amazing thing that has ever happened to you? How did it feel? Did you find it difficult to believe? Was it an exhilarating experience – or devastating? Sometimes we just cannot think rationally about these occasions. Our feelings simply overwhelm us and bypass our thought processes. So what about the most important thing that has ever happened? It is important to be ready for the sheer excitement, wonder, amazement and joy which is now to be unleashed. Be ready for running to empty tombs, surprise encounters, emotional reunions, gratitude and shame, reflection and forgiveness. Reading doesn't come much more emotional than this.

READ John 20,21

INTO THE BIBLE

Who was the first to reach the empty tomb (20:1,2), the first to meet Jesus (20:10–18) and the first to be sent out by him to tell others (20:17,18)? What a privilege!

What do you think convinced the 'other disciple' and caused him to believe (20:8)? Clearly it wasn't that he had suddenly understood 'Scripture' (20:9)!

JOHN'S GOSPEL

At first, the risen Lord was not recognised by Mary (20:13–15). Do you think this was simply because of her grief and tears or because Jesus had taken on a resurrection body and looked slightly different (see 1 Corinthians 15:35–44)?

What were the main things Jesus did as he met up with his disciples?

Thomas finally expresses the ultimate confession of a disciple (20:28). Do you feel that objective 'proof' is necessary to be a real disciple?

As ever, the risen Jesus meets his disciples where they are – just as he had before. Compare John 21:1–14 with Luke 5:1–11. What has changed in between these two occasions?

GOD AND YOU

- Mary's encounter with Jesus is very emotional and his response seems to recognise that. Like one of his favoured sheep (10:16), she hears him and recognises his voice as he speaks her name. How much do you allow emotion to enter your relationship with Jesus?

- **John 20:24–29** Thomas has appeared before in John's Gospel (11:16; 14:5). What clues can you see in his earlier words that might make you think he is the archetypal doubter? In what ways does your character or personality affect your faith in Jesus?

- Simon Peter had let Jesus down badly (18:15–27), though not in the same way as Judas (13:18–30; 18:5). In what ways does Jesus make his forgiveness and reinstatement of Simon obvious and personal (21:15–23)? How does that make *you* feel?

INTO ACTION

Is there any sense in which you need to rediscover Jesus at the place you were in when you first met him (21:1–14; Luke 5:1–11)? Think about how and why you first started to follow Jesus. Realise afresh your relationship with him – take time to do that now.

Forgiveness is central to the gospel (look also at Luke 15:11–32; 23:34,42,43). Are there any people you need either to forgive or be forgiven by? And in what ways might you need to seek God's forgiveness? Jesus, after all, taught us to do both regularly (Matthew 6:12).

Extra

> Read 1 Corinthians 15 for more about the resurrection of Christ and what it means for Christians.

BIRD'S EYE VIEW

JOHN'S GOSPEL

So, what *is* God like? John could have offered us a fine philosophy with lots of intellectual analysis and definitions. But when God wanted to show what he was really like, he chose to live amongst us and share our lives (1:14). This happened with the real flesh and blood life of Jesus. As Thomas said as Jesus stood before him, 'My LORD and my God!' (20:28).

WHAT'S GOD LIKE?

Look back over Jesus' encounters with individuals, his debates with inquirers and opponents, his miraculous signs and, most especially, his death and resurrection. Looking at these, what would you say Jesus showed us about his Father God?

THREE-IN-ONE

John is very important for our understanding of the Trinity. After Jesus had gone back to heaven it took the church a good deal more time to work it all out – and we still have lots to talk about. But John provides plenty of raw material.

What does John tell us about Jesus as God's Son – the one who is perfectly obedient and submissive to his Father? Remind yourself by looking back through John's Gospel. God the Father is often in the background of John's account throughout.

What does Jesus say about the Holy Spirit and their relationship? Look again at John 14–16 especially. Although Jesus is set to depart and return to his Father, he tells his disciples that they will not be left as orphans (14:18). Jesus will still be with them, but they will experience him in the person of his Spirit. The Father, Son and Spirit will be together with the disciples and continue to live a life dependent upon each other. Look back too at the wonderful prayer and promise which Jesus prays for us in John 17:20–26.

MORE ABOUT GOD

- Look back over your reading of the Gospel and pick out one incident which struck you forcibly when you first read it. How does it fit in with the rest of the Gospel as you now know it? Have your views on it changed? Now you know about the whole book, how does that contribute to your understanding of that particular incident?

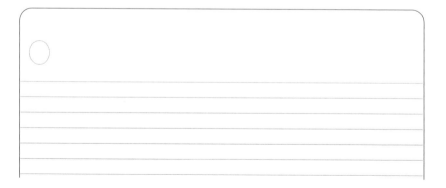

JOHN'S GOSPEL

- Go back to a favourite character with whom you were fascinated or felt a kind of identity. How do you think John uses this character to express ideas which run through the whole Gospel?

- At the beginning we said that John seems to stand outside of his story and view it as a whole. Now you've read his Gospel through, do you agree with this? What difference does that make to John's story?

- Did you notice all Jesus' miraculous signs and 'I am' statements? There are seven of each. See if you can find them all. Write them in the journal space, then spend time meditating on one or two of them. How might these sum up what John is trying to teach us about God?

- John leaves us with a lot of very powerful images and pictures. Write some of them down. Let them take root in your imagination and feed your thinking about what God is like. Allow his Spirit to be at work in you as you grow in your knowledge of him day by day.

PSALMS 1–41: WHAT'S GOD LIKE?

The Big Picture

What music do you enjoy listening to at the moment? Whether it's classical or contemporary, music is really powerful: it can move you, change your mood and stay with you long after you hit the 'pause' button. Whether you're a skilled musician or just love losing yourself in someone else's art, music will probably be a strong influence throughout your life.

Right in the middle of the Bible, there are 150 songs. The tunes may have been lost to us, but the lyrics still sing out!

SONGS OF SIGNIFICANCE

We're going to focus on the first book of Psalms: Psalms 1–41. Apart from Psalm 1, they are all thought to be written by David, and so originally date from around 1000 BC. There's some debate about whether the 'A psalm of David' inscription might sometimes mean *for* David or *in the style* of David, but we're going to assume they are his work. And that's significant: first, because David's music seems to have had spiritual power (1 Samuel 16:14–23); and second, because the words of someone whom God calls 'a man after my own heart' (Acts 13:22) must be worth hearing, don't you think?!

David's psalms have had a massive impact, way beyond his own lifetime and walk with God: they became the temple hymnbook in Old Testament times; Jesus himself used them (Matthew 27:46); the apostles and New Testament writers frequently quoted from them (eg Acts 2:25–35; Hebrews 1:5); they have been recited in churches throughout history – and you'll find lines from the Psalms in even the most up to date worship songs!

These songs give us lots of insights into the character of David, but more important than this, they tell us about the God in whom David trusted. As we'll see, this is a God who could sustain David through the darkest times and cause him to sing for joy even when the whole world seemed to be against him.

Extra

> Spend some time reviewing your own collection of hymns or contemporary worship songs; choose songs which speak most strongly to and for you.

PSALMS 1–41

THINK ABOUT...

Spend some time thinking about how, at this moment, you might answer the question, 'What's God like?' You might like to jot down your thoughts in the journal space. When you've finished reading these psalms, you could look back at what you've said here and add anything new that you've discovered.

SONGS OF THE HEART

There's nothing restrained or private about David's spirituality and he is as passionate in his anger and disappointment as he is effusive in his praise and thanksgiving. You are guaranteed to find something in the Psalms which resonates powerfully with your own life experience; they may be ancient songs, but much has stayed the same.

Remember, though, that in a very real way *everything* has changed: David based his relationship with God on his own record of obedience and trust (eg Psalm 17:1–5); ours is founded on Christ alone (Romans 3:21–31).

THINK ABOUT...

'... the Psalms were meant to be sung, danced or wept – not primarily studied' (Alan Palmer, *Psalms 1–72*, Crossways Bible Guide Series, Crossway Books, 1996). As you begin this series, prepare yourself to engage more than just your mind. Be ready to feel – and express those feelings. Be ready to release your creativity.

Extra

Before you hear the songs, take some time to read the story of David's life. It starts at 1 Samuel 16, continues through 2 Samuel, and ends with his death in 1 Kings 2:10. There'll be some very familiar stories – and some which may surprise you.

BEGIN

To whet your appetite, read Psalm 1. In the journal space, note anything you find striking about it.

1 Our awesome God

PSALMS 1–41

GET READY

What causes you to stop and think, 'You are amazing, God…'?

Why not choose a song which helps you praise God and sing it out to him now? You might want to use a CD version or just your own voice (which doesn't, by the way, need to be great in order to bring God pleasure!). Let the song inspire you to praise God in your own words.

READ Psalms 2, 8, 15, 19, 24, 29, 33

As you read…

INTO THE BIBLE

…note down (through word, image or symbol) what makes David stand in awe of God. You might find it helpful to use the theme headings below:

God and creation

God and world powers

God and us

God's instructions for living

God's character

GOD AND YOU

Choose as many as you like from the options which follow.

- You might be living in a fast-paced, technological, urban world, but creation can still speak volumes to you about God's brilliant mind, his attention to detail and his power! Look again at David's reflections on creation in Psalms 8; 19:1–6; 29 and 33:1–9. What experiences of the natural world have made an impact on you? Perhaps it's a place you've visited, something you work on or study, or maybe you're watching a child grow. Paste an image of whatever is meaningful for you in the journaling space. What does it show you about God? Spend time really thinking about that, then address your thoughts to God. You could craft them into your own psalm or poem, if you like.

- Are you as enthusiastic as David about what God requires of you? Be honest with God about any areas of your life in which you are struggling to be obedient. Reread Psalm 19:7–11 and consider how bringing your life into line with what God wants could be life-enhancing – not restricting. Make a note of what you say to God and what actions you will take. You might also like to use Psalm 19:12–14 as your own prayer.

PSALMS 1–41

- What does David say about God's character in this collection of Psalms? Some things are implied, such as his holiness in Psalms 15 and 24; some things are overtly stated, as in Psalm 33:4,5. Use the journaling space to note down times in your life when you've been especially aware of those characteristics. What else has your life shown you about what God is like? Spend time telling God what you appreciate about him.

INTO ACTION

In Psalm 2, 24:1 and 33:10–19, David speaks confidently about God's supreme authority over world events. As you watch the news this week, does it *seem* to you that God is in overall control? How would it help you – and how might it challenge you – to view the world as David did? Talk with God about this.

Extra

Psalms 15 and 24 are 'entrance liturgies'. They were probably composed to commemorate David bringing the ark of the covenant to Jerusalem. Check out 2 Samuel 6:1–19; 1 Chronicles 13:1–14 and 15:25 – 16:6 for the full story.

2 The God who listens

GET READY

Which of these statements is closest to how you feel about your life at the moment?

☐ Everything's great!

☐ There are some good things… and some problems.

☐ There's a big issue which is overshadowing everything else.

In this session – and the next – the focus is on David's songs for hard times. They may seem absolutely relevant to you right now, or not relevant at all. Even if you ticked the 'Everything's great!' box, be ready to let these psalms speak to you anyway. You might use them to help someone close to you and, you never know, you *may* need them yourself one day.

READ Psalms 6, 12, 17, 22, 26, 28, 35, 38, 39

Get hold of some pens or pencils in a range of colours. As you read you could use different colours to highlight David's different emotions (eg red to represent anger and so on).

INTO THE BIBLE

What issues is David struggling with in these psalms?

How would you describe the way he expresses himself?

Does anything he says surprise you? Or jar with you?

PSALMS 1–41

GOD AND YOU

Choose as many as you like from the options which follow.

- What tends to happen to your walk with God when life is tough? Read Psalms 6, 35 and 38 again, being aware of how David relates to God in hard times. What similarities – or differences – are there between your approach and his?

- If you are facing a difficult issue, talk with God about it now. Speak with the same honesty and openness that David had, making your requests clear. Go back into the Psalms and use any phrases which express how you are feeling (eg Psalms 6:3; 22:2). Make a note of what you say to God – and what you hear from him (eg Psalm 12:5).

- Psalm 22 is extraordinary. It so clearly points to Jesus' suffering on the cross (Matthew 27:35,39,43; John 19:23,24,28). Jesus quotes it aloud from the cross (Matthew 27:46) and commentators suggest that he probably recited all of it, silently, as he died there. Reread Psalm 22 and talk with Jesus about the light it sheds on what he went through – for you. Rejoice in the words of verse 31!

- David's view of his enemies may sometimes seem vindictive (eg Psalm 28:4,5; 35). However, it does reveal an important truth: God can be trusted to deal with those who hurt us. In the light of this, think about any broken relationships in your own life. How does it help to recognise that God knows all about each one of those situations and the people involved?

INTO ACTION

David's concerns are often personal, but if you review Psalms 12 and 28:9, you'll see he engages with God about national issues too. How about you? Watch a news bulletin on the TV or online, or look through your newspaper in God's company. Speak with him – *cry out* to him! – about the issues which strike you. Maybe you could paste an image or a headline in the journaling space here as a record of your conversation.

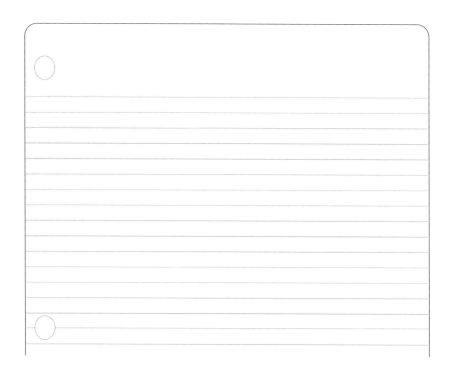

3 The God you can trust

PSALMS 1–41

GET READY

Take a few minutes to review the previous session. Remind yourself of what you said to God – and how you said it. What difference has that conversation made?

An honest expression of how David sees the difficult situations in his life, plus bold requests to God for help, are both key elements of the songs he wrote in hard times. But that's not all.

READ Psalms 3, 4, 5, 10, 13, 25, 31, 41

Focus on the more upbeat things David has to say. As you read…

INTO THE BIBLE

…note down the words and phrases which strike you for each of the three statements below:

In spite of everything, I *am* confident (eg Psalm 25:15)…

…because I *know* what God is like (eg Psalm 5:4);

…because I'm secure in my relationship with him (eg Psalm 31:15).

GOD AND YOU

Choose as many as you like from the options which follow.

- In the end, it's our relationship with God that really matters. David's freedom to be real with God in a crisis (eg Psalm 13:1,2) and his ability to rejoice even before he's seen it resolved (eg Psalm 13:5) reveal a man who trusts God deeply, knows God intimately and is genuinely secure with him. What is your relationship with God like? What do your reactions to life's difficult times say about how well you know him?

- Reflect on what *you* can say with confidence about God himself and about how he does things. Find and use phrases from the Psalms which you can speak out – and really mean – as a starting point.

- Consider what you can say with confidence about where you stand with God, borrowing any of David's phrases which speak for you. What help do you need in feeling secure about this? Is there anything *you* need to do to build your relationship with him?

- Record your thoughts, statements and favourite quotations in the journaling space. Then speak them out to God.

PSALMS 1–41

INTO ACTION

If you are facing a difficult issue, use David's psalms to help you continue your conversation with God about it: perhaps create your own psalm in his style; or choose a psalm which seems especially appropriate for your own situation and rewrite it in your own words – or set it to music, or paint it, or dance it.

Focus on someone close to you, for whom life is tough right now. Consider prayerfully how you can support them emotionally, practically and spiritually.

Tim Hughes writes:

> 'One evening I sat with my guitar and poured out my heart to God. I found great hope and strength being able to express my pain, and in the midst of the doubt, singing, "I will praise you, I will praise you, when the tears fall still I will sing to you."
>
> 'Life is full of pain and sorrow. Loved ones die, dreams fail, people get hurt – we are left with unanswered questions. That's the reality of the world we live in. Yet in the midst of the pain, through the tears, God is good. He is and always will be worthy of our praise.'

Reproduced by permission from Survivor Records, written by Tim Hughes, and taken from *When Silence Falls*. www.survivor.co.uk

4 God of action

GET READY

In the journal space opposite create a 'timeline' to represent your life so far. You might draw a line across or around the page – or it might be a spiral or circles. Then add the main events so far, using key words or symbols. Now add where and how you've been aware of God working in your life at different times. What has he done *specifically* for *you*?

READ Psalms 9, 18, 21, 30, 32, 34, 40

Praise God as you read David's exuberant songs of thanksgiving.

INTO THE BIBLE

Who do you think David is talking to in these psalms? Compare, for example, Psalm 9:1–6 with Psalms 9:11; 30:4,5 and 34:3.

Notice the different word pictures David uses to describe God (eg Psalm 9:9 and 18:2). Meditate on one or two of them. What do they actually communicate about God?

GOD AND YOU

Choose as many as you like from the options which follow.

- How do you view hardship when it hits your life? From the other side of a crisis, David has some useful insights. Look again at Psalms 18:33–36; 30:5; 34:19; 40:1–3. How does each statement inform and challenge your own view of a difficult situation you are in now, or have had, in your own life? Talk with God about this.

Draw your timeline here.

PSALMS 1–41

- Reread Psalm 32. Have you ever experienced that before-and-after feeling as you've allowed God to deal with wrongdoing in your own life? Spend some time in God's presence, allowing the Holy Spirit to make you aware of anything you need to own up to now.

- How good are you at waiting? Look at Psalm 40:1 in the light of anything God has yet to answer or resolve in your life. Talk with God about the delay between bringing something to him in prayer and seeing his response.

- You probably don't have human enemies to contend with in the same way David did! But what *does* come against you (Ephesians 6:12)? What does Psalm 18:37–50 show us about our partnership with God in seeing our enemies defeated? Talk with God about any battles you are facing. Be aware of what you need to do – and ask God to do what *only he* can do.

PSALMS 1–41

INTO ACTION

Look back at your timeline (page 55). What stories do *you* have to tell of God's goodness? Write some in the journaling space here. You might find David's psalm structure, as below, helpful.

God has...

Now I see that God is...

And that he will...

Tell your story to God first – but don't stop there! David thanked God in front of an audience as a way of leading people to worship. Isn't it encouraging to hear what God is doing in people's lives *now*? So, take the initiative. With whom can you share your story? And how? Go ahead and actually do it! If your story stays within the pages of this journal, you'll have missed half the point (Psalm 40:3).

5 The God who longs to bless

GET READY

Have you seen the film *Sliding Doors*? It's a pretty standard romantic comedy, except that it weaves together two different stories: one plays out the scenario of Helen *just* catching a tube train, and so meeting her man; and in the other we watch what happens if she misses the train. The film lets us see that even trivial, everyday decisions can have huge consequences. We're not always aware of it, but our choices, attitudes and actions *always* lead us somewhere.

READ Psalms 1, 7, 11, 14, 16, 20, 23, 27, 36, 37

Decisions and their consequences are a key theme in Psalm 1 and in David's songs of trust and wisdom. As you read…

INTO THE BIBLE

…notice the attitudes, actions or beliefs described by David – and their consequences. There's lots about 'the wicked', but just focus for now on those which apply to God's people, for example, if God is my light, then I have nothing to fear (Psalm 27:1).

Go back and highlight those which speak directly to you.

PSALMS 1–41

GOD AND YOU

Now choose as many as you like from the options below.

- David is quite clear about which actions and attitudes lead to life, and which do not. Take your time with this (make yourself a coffee or whatever) and sit in God's company with these psalms. Psalm 1 teaches us the benefits of meditating on God's Word, of *really* thinking about it and letting its truth sink deeply into us. So try that: ask yourself if those attitudes, beliefs or actions are in you. If so, are you *really* living in the good of their consequences? Commit especially relevant verses to heart so that they live with you throughout your day.

- What's also striking in these psalms is the contrast between the life experience and destiny of those who trust in God – and those who don't. New Testament teaching echoes this, but it's easy for us to forget this. Talk with God about those people you know and love who are living their lives without him. Let your heart be moved to pray and act towards their salvation.

- When David sings about his life, it's often with an eternal perspective. What difference could it make to your life *now* to know you'll 'dwell in the house of the LORD forever' (Psalm 23:6) and enjoy eternal pleasures at his right hand (Psalm 16:11)?

INTO ACTION

Psalm 23 is probably one of the best known Bible texts of all time – but don't let familiarity dull its impact! Its rich imagery describes the blessings of living under God's authority and guidance. Engage with it creatively by setting it to music, or dramatising it, or depicting it visually, using film or computer technology – whatever your gift. Present whatever you do to God, as your way of saying this psalm to him.

Pray Psalm 20:1–5 for someone close to you. Then text, e-mail or send it to them.

BIRD'S EYE VIEW

PSALMS 1–41

We've heard the anthems of a man who not only knew God well, but who also invited and expected God to examine and know about every area of his life. For David, no area of life was outside God's interest, no emotion 'off limits'. His songs *are* beautiful – but they're also raw and real. Spend time in God's company thinking about how David's life can spur you on to become *more* of a man or woman after his own heart (Acts 13:22).

Make a few notes in the journal space to sum up what you've discovered from David about…

    sources of inspiration for praising God;

    relating to God in times of trouble;

    responding to God's work in your life;

    which attitudes and actions to cultivate, and which to let go.

SING OUT FOR GOD

Choose as many as you like from the options which follow.

- If you ever lead a crowd or small group of children or adults in worship, spend time talking with God about that ministry: the gift of it, the privilege of it, the challenge of it. Have David's psalms inspired you to approach things differently? How could you encourage people to 'sing joyfully' (Psalm 33:1), 'play skilfully' (Psalm 33:3), 'sing to him a *new* song' (Psalm 33:3) and 'ascribe to the LORD glory and strength' (Psalm 29:1)?

- If, like David, you are a creative person, spend time talking with God about the talents he has given you. What opportunities do you have to use them? What new possibilities might you pursue?

- According to David, one of the hallmarks of the ungodly person is a callous disregard for the needs of the poor and oppressed (Psalm 37:14). God, David says, cares for and defends those in need in our community (Psalms 9:9; 10:14,17,18; 35:10). The implication? So should we. In what ways are you involved in being an agent for God to bring about social justice nationally and internationally? Is there more you could and should be doing? Talk with God about this now.

PSALMS 1–41

- David's art has outlived him. How many millions of people have taken *his* words to express the cry of their own hearts? And here's the truth: you and I are also chosen for 'fruit that will last' (John 15:16). It's not always easy to think beyond the right here and right now, but what are you building for the future? Are you investing in something that will have an impact beyond your generation?

- Write your own psalm for God. Think about what you'd like to say to him at this time in your life. Do you have questions to ask, requests to make or anxieties to air? Do you want to say what you love about him or what you know to be true? Spend time working with your words, crafting them to express exactly what you want to say. When it's ready, speak it out to God – and record it here.

Enjoyed this title in the **Bible Max** series?

If you'd like to read more, look out for

Journeys with God

- Get the big picture of God's story as you read big 'chunks' of his Word.
- 15 more sessions to help you on your own journey with God as you read about his people in **Genesis** and **Ruth**.
- Includes space for journaling to help you reflect and grow as you spend more time with God.

JOURNEYS WITH GOD

£4.99

Available through your local Christian bookshop.

Order by phone: 0845 07 06 006

or online: www.scriptureunion.org.uk